Grip of Heaven

Grip of Heaven.
Copyright © 2022 by H. Bruce Buolton.

All rights reserved. No part of this book may be reproduced in any form or by any electronic or mechanical means, including information storage and retrieval systems, without permission in writing from the publisher and author, except by reviewers, who may quote brief passages in a review.

This publication contains the opinions and ideas of its author. It is intended to provide helpful and informative material on the subjects addressed in the publication. The author and publisher specifically disclaim all responsibility for any liability, loss, or risk, personal or otherwise, which is incurred as a consequence, directly or indirectly, of the use and application of any of the contents of this book.

ISBN: 978-1-63950-129-8   [Paperback Edition]
        978-1-63950-130-4   [eBook Edition]

Printed and bound in The United States of America.

Gateway Towards Success

1309 Coffeen Avenue
STE 1200, Sheridan,
Wyoming, 82801 USA

+13179780258 | www.writersapex.com

H. BRUCE BOULTON

GRIP
of Heaven

Second Edition

CONTENTS

Contents 5
Prologue 6
Dedication 8

Chapter 1:	My Great Awakening	10
Chapter 2:	Revelation	17
Chapter 3:	Seeing and Hearing	22
Chapter 4:	The Nakedness Principle	26
Chapter 5:	The Battlefield of the Mind	29
Chapter 6:	Angels	31
Chapter 7:	The Meat Hook Principle	33
Chapter 8:	The Promised Land	35
Chapter 9:	Communion	41
Chapter 10:	My Hiding Place	45
Chapter 11:	Gold and Silver Nuggets	47
Chapter 12:	Baptized with the Holy Spirit	48

PROLOGUE

The title *Grip of Heaven* came from a vision the Lord gave me following my precious Annie's homegoing in November 2016. She exhibited a real peace of mind in the few weeks prior to her passing that gave no evidence of her physical condition or circumstances. I discovered the source of that peace in the months following as I searched her personal belongings. I found a scribbled note on her coupon envelope in her pocketbook that read, "Stop holding on and be held by Jesus." Later, I read in her journal, "I saw a roadside sign that said, 'Stop holding on and be held by the loving arms of Jesus.' So much of this applies to me."

I observed her inner peace during her last days and especially during her nine-day stay in the hospital. My vision of the pierced hand of Jesus gripping Ann's hand came soon after this discovery. With it came encouragement to write this book and tell others of the walk she and I had walked over the last forty-five years following our Lord's leading in all aspects of our lives together.

My desire is that we all accept His will for our lives now as we pray the Lord's Prayer in Matthew 6:10: "Thy kingdom come. Thy will be done, on earth as it is in heaven." The kingdom is the Holy Spirit's rule in our souls—our minds, emotions, and wills. Matthew 6:33 tells us to "seek first His kingdom," Matthew 3:2 reads, "is at hand," and Luke 17:21 reads, "within you." The earth is my soul, not the round ball we walk on. Genesis 2:7 tells us God formed humanity from dust. And Matthew 5:13 tells us, "You are the salt of the earth."

I am greatly encouraged as I journey through life as a seeker of truth by a quote from page 37 of George H. Warnock's book *Beauty for Ashes Part 1* "The Family of God" section.

> If this is the day of the unveiling of Christ, and the joining together of the Body of Christ, it is also the day of the UNVEILING OF THE HUMAN HEART, and the manifestation of the hidden things of darkness that lie concealed in the hearts of God's people.

All scripture references come from the *New American Standard Bible Reference Edition*, 1973.

I also offer quotes from Ann's and my favorite daily devotional book, *My Utmost for His Highest* by Oswald Chambers, the updated edition of 1992. I will use *OC* as the abbreviation for this source.

DEDICATION

My precious wife, Ann Hopkins Boulton, whom I always called my Annie, is the only person I can dedicate this book to. She was the most loving and giving woman I have ever known. She was that way since the day I met her.

We met at Alfred University in 1956, her senior year and my junior year. She and I waited on table at The Brick, a woman's dorm, to pay for our meal plans. She and I were dating other people at that time, but we found we could talk with each other about the difficulties we were having with those relationships.

We enjoyed the freedom to discuss anything and began to build a relationship that encouraged each of us to break up with those we had been dating. We were almost like sister and brother at the beginning, but then, we began to think more seriously about a long-term relationship.

She seemed to know I was the right one for her before I came to the same conclusion. I asked for a time of separation to sort things out. I later learned she had told her roommate that if I wasn't the one, she wanted someone just like me.

She didn't hang onto me—she left me free to make my own decision about our relationship. That was the best thing she could have done; it sent me directly to the Lord for my help in making a decision.

A note here. If you live by the openhanded principle, you don't hang onto things and situations and the Lord's hand is then free to control the situation.

Annie graduated in June 1957 and went to work as a nurse in New Jersey. I started my senior year at Alfred that fall. We were planning a June 1958 wedding after I had graduated, and we were discussing honeymoon destinations. All things were proceeding well until we looked into the possibility of a February wedding and a start to our marriage at Alfred. It happened. She found a job working in the infirmary on campus, and I had my job waiting on table for meals. On February 1, 1958, we married. We found a nice apartment, and her parents let us use their second car for six months.

It was interesting to read in the newspapers reports of our wedding that for our honeymoon, we had motored through New York State. In truth, we simply drove back to the university.

I miss my Annie very much, but she's in a better place now; she is in no pain and is at peace. I talk with her every day as if she were here with me. We are soul mates who will never be separated.

Thank you, Lord Jesus, for the beautiful wife you gave me, amen.

CHAPTER 1

My Great Awakening

In 1970, Ann and I decided to leave our jobs in corporate sales. I had spent twelve years working in that field. Our children were growing up, and I wasn't around home as much as I wanted. I was supposed to be the father of my family; that was the main reason for that big change in our lives.

We moved back to Upstate New York after selling our New Jersey home and settled into a nice, new home in Clifton Park. I began working in my father's real estate appraising business and got busy fulfilling the educational requirements I needed to be successful in that field. As was our normal practice, we joined the local RCA—the Reformed Church in America—and followed our usual pattern of joining the choir and teaching Sunday school.

At that church, we observed an elder who seemed to be on fire for the Lord, which was a new experience for Ann and me.

The elder's name was Gene. He went to Detroit for a denominational conference on evangelism. He told me that prior to his trip, one of his daughters had asked him if he was prejudiced against blacks. He said, "Yes, I think so. I wouldn't want a black family to buy a home next to me for fear that the value of my home would be affected negatively."

Well, when he arrived at the conference in Detroit, he found that those at the conference were predominately black Christian men and women and that a well-known black Christian was the main speaker.

Following that conference, Gene was powerfully convicted of his prejudice by the Holy Spirit. As he explained it, he felt like a bucket of honey had been poured over him, and as it dripped past his eyes, tears of repentance began to flow. He was overcome by a love he had not experienced before. All prejudice was gone and had been replaced by a love so special that he never wanted it to go away. That love was manifest in his activity in our little church. I would jokingly say that he would jump over pews to pray with people. And many prayers for healing were answered.

This was in the early seventies, when the charismatic renewal was just coming to our area. Ann and I attended a conference called Celebration of Good News at a local university. Ann was very impressed by a Catholic priest praying without a prayer book as if he had a personal relationship with God. Ann, whose background was Episcopalian, had never seen that before. She and I asked a group leader how we could learn what that was all about, and he suggested we read Watchman Nee's book *Release of the Spirit*. We used that book and other books by Nee as a foundation for our journey in the Spirit, and I still refer to them today.

One experience we had at this "lively" time at our church was the formation of a group of couples who gathered Friday evenings to share our lives' happenings, sing hymns, and pray for each other. We called ourselves the Strugglers; our primary question was whether there was something more to this Christian life than just the time spent from ten to eleven o'clock on Sunday mornings.

Our pastor did not encourage us in this endeavor. He didn't come to our Friday-evening meetings, and I didn't know why. I had a difficult time talking with him about spiritual things; he seemed uncomfortable outside the pulpit, where he always preached from notes. I don't remember him mentioning any personal experiences when he preached. Those were the circumstances surrounding what happened next.

One Friday evening, I was in charge of our group; that was a responsibility we changed each week. We heard a knock on the door; our pastor had come with his wife—a surprise. We of course welcomed them to join us.

During the evening as we shared our week's experiences, a man sitting next to the pastor said that Gene, the elder who was on fire for the Lord, had prayed for his daughter to be healed (from what ailment I don't remember) and that she had been healed. We were sharing similar testimonies when our pastor's wife began to cry and exclaim that we were going to drive them out of the ministry. The pastor joined in with his complaints.

I have no memory of that evening other than the confusion that unfolded and the meeting breaking up hastily. Ann and I left that night with confusion in our minds and many questions.

That's the night I had my great awakening in a dream. I woke up and went down to our living room. I saw my Bible opened on the couch. I hadn't left it there. It was open to Galatians 5, and verses 16–24 seemed to be illuminated. I picked up the Bible and read the verses.

> But I say, walk by the Spirit, and you will not carry out desire of the flesh. For the flesh sets its desire against the Spirit, and the Spirit against the flesh; for these are in opposition to one another, so that you may not do the things that you please. But if you are led by the Spirit, you are not under the Law. Now the deeds of the flesh are evident, which are: immorality, impurity, sensuality, idolatry, sorcery, enmities, strife jealousy, OUTBURSTS OF ANGER,

DISPUTES, DISSENSIONS, FACTIONS, envyings, drunkenness, carousings, and things like these, of which I forewarn you just as I have forewarned you that those who practice such things shall not inherit the kingdom of God. But the fruit of the Spirit is love, joy, peace, patience, kindness, goodness, faithfulness, gentleness, self-control; against such things there is no law. Now those who belong to Christ Jesus have crucified the flesh with its passions and desires.

Those capitalized words were emphasized; they were the pastor's and his wife's responses, but I couldn't understand them. In my mind, pastors should never act like that—they were trained in seminary to be understanding, kind, and in control of their negative emotions so not to offend people. For some reason, I put pastors on a mental pedestal; they were never supposed to be offensive. I've since found a word that better describes it: *sacrosanct*, which *Webster's* defines as very sacred, holy, or inviolable.

I went back upstairs, and my wife was waking up. I told her that I would speak with the pastor and that everything would be okay.

When I drove up the driveway to the church, the pastor walked out the front door, opened my car door, got in, and began to pour out his anxieties and hurts for a number of minutes. I said we should go next door and talk to his wife; I knew she was also upset. He agreed, and we went and talked for a few minutes. Then I said I would get Gene and we would all work this out.

I drove to Gene's. He was raking leaves. I got out of my car, and he dropped the rake, came over, and gave me a big hug. That was the first time I had been hugged like that by a man. We talked about what was happening, and we drove back to the parsonage, went in, talked everything over, asked for forgiveness, hugged each other, and left.

And then I woke up—it was morning. Just as in the dream, I went downstairs and saw the Bible open where I had not left it, and the day began to unfold exactly as it had in my dream.

One of the physical manifestations of what happened to me that day was the shedding of tears that seemed to never end. That's when I began to call myself a "leaky" Christian. I was in the real estate business and had a purchase offer to present that afternoon, so I tried to dry my wet, red eyes by opening the window of my car as I drove. I wanted to be presentable for my meeting.

I spent many months enjoying my spiritual awakening as Ann and I shared our new lives together—meetings, conferences, late-night prayer meetings, and so on. Then, I began to think about that dream and my new walk in the Spirit. I boldly asked the Holy Spirit what He thought had happened to me as a result of my dream.

The Holy Spirit said to me, "I want to teach you about the born-again experience that I shared with Nicodemus." The setting appeared to be a classroom with Him as the instructor. I never saw Him, but I heard His voice clearly. In front of me was an anatomy book open to the section covering pregnancy and birth with overlays that showed a pregnant woman. Each overlay was opened until I saw the baby in the womb.

He said, "I want to talk to you about physical birth first. I have two parts of My creation come together during intercourse—the sperm and the egg. Each is perfectly made to accomplish My purpose, and as they join, a miracle of My making happens—new life is formed, and from that moment, taking of that life is murder."

My fuzziness about when life began and the abortion fight going on disappeared.

"Then the baby grows for approximately nine months and is born."

He said that being born was an earthly experience that involved the feelings and emotions of all parties involved.

He said, "I want to share with you the spiritual counterpart of this birthing experience. It is very similar to the physical in that I take two parts of My creation—the human spirit and My Holy Spirit—and as they are joined, when My plan for salvation or regeneration through My Son, Jesus, is accepted—that He died on the cross as the only perfect sacrifice for the sin of humanity—a miracle of My making takes place, and new spiritual life is created that can never be done away with.

"I put My Holy Spirit in your spirit. It is similar to the physical experience known as conception with the exception that no one can undo what I have done. This is the 'born of water' word I spoke to Nicodemus about. Spiritual water is the same as eternal life."

He referred me to John 4 and the woman at the well.

"After salvation or regeneration has occurred," He said, "sometimes instantly, but sometimes nine seconds, or nine minutes, hours, days, months, years and sometimes never is that new, eternal life is born into the kingdom of heaven on earth. I'm speaking of the 'born of the Spirit' section of John 3:5."

He referred me to John 20:22, when He breathed on the disciples and said to them, "Receive the Holy Spirit." That's when they were born of water—eternal life. He sent me to Acts 1:5: "But you shall be baptized with the Holy Spirit not many days from now." That's when they were born of the Spirit. He reminded me that birthing experiences on earth involved the feelings and emotions of all parties concerned. He said, "Remember Pentecost. The dream I gave you was your 'born of the Spirit,' your empowerment experience. I called you to be a peacemaker."

He gave me a visual aid to illustrate the born-again experience.

> After I was saved [born of water], I was walking in the tunnel of religious doctrine. Everything was the color red all around me, and as I walked along, a church doctrine or idea would come at me in written form, and if I liked it, I would grab onto it until another came along that I also liked or was better than the previous one. I'd grab onto it and discard the one it replaced. The color red represents My blood and took me to Romans 5:9, "… having now been justified by His blood."
>
> In the next section of the vision, I was outside the tunnel and in the midst of brilliant light. I had unlimited vision in all directions. I looked back and saw in the distance the tunnel I had been released from.

I had a beautiful illustration of what my "born of the Spirit" experience looked like after His explanation of it through this teaching vision. Matthew 13:16 reads, "But blessed are your eyes, because they see; and your ears, because they hear."

CHAPTER 2

Revelation

In Matthew 16:16–19, we read,

> And Simon Peter answered and said, "Thou art the Christ, the Son of the living God." And Jesus answered and said to him, "Blessed are you, Simon Barjonas, because flesh and blood did not reveal this to you, but My Father who is in heaven. And I also say to you that you are Peter, and upon this rock I will build My church; and the gates of Hades shall not overpower it. I will give you the keys of the kingdom of heaven; and whatever you shall bind on earth shall have been bound in heaven, and whatever you shall loose on earth shall have been loosed in heaven."

I'd like to offer some insight I received from the Holy Spirit about these scriptures. Peter heard from the Holy Spirit, not natural wisdom or flesh and blood, that Jesus was indeed the Christ, the Son of the Living God. The church is being built on revelation from

Jesus's Father, who is in heaven. The church has no existence apart from the revelation of Jesus Christ.

In 1 Corinthians 10:4, we read, "The rock was Jesus." Psalm 118:22–23 tells us, "The stone which the builders rejected Has become the chief corner stone. This is the Lord's doing; It is marvelous in our eyes."

Peter experienced spiritual revelation or an anointing from Jesus's heavenly Father in His spirit. Jesus is the door between the natural and the spiritual: "I am the door" (John 10:19).

> But you have an anointing from the Holy One and you all know. And as for you, the anointing which you received from Him abides in you, and you have no need for any one to teach you: but as His anointing teaches you about all things, and is true and is not a lie, and just as it taught you, you abide in Him. (1 John 2:20, 27)

> ... that the God of our Lord Jesus Christ, the Father of glory, may give to you a spirit of wisdom and of revelation in the knowledge of Him. (Ephesians 1:17)

> You search the Scriptures, because you think that in them you have eternal life; and it is these that bear witness of Me. (John 5:39)

In reference to the "keys of the kingdom of heaven," I see in the scripture the basis or foundation of all the truths I have come to know in my walk in the Spirit.

> Now may the God of peace Himself sanctify you entirely; and may your spirit and soul and body be preserved complete, without blame at the coming of our Lord Jesus Christ. Faithful is He who calls you, and He also will bring it to pass. (1 Thessalonians 5:23–24)

This is where the binding and loosing of Matthew 16:19 took place.

My spirit was sanctified when I accepted Christ as my Savior. His Spirit filled my spirit, and Hebrews 13:5 states, "I will never desert you, nor will I ever forsake you." My spirit is now ready for heaven when He is ready to take me home.

> My sheep hear my voice, and I know them, and they follow Me; and I give eternal life to them; and they shall never perish, and no one shall snatch them out of My hand. My Father, who has given them to Me, is greater than all; and no one is able to snatch them out of the Father's hand. (John 10:27–29)

The sanctification of the soul (mind, emotions and will; I call this my control center), takes a lifetime and is accomplished one day at a time. The daily bread, the situations the Lord brings into my life each day, exposes my old nature under the law of sin and death and gives me the choice to bind it to my life or loose it, crucify it, let it go from my life so it doesn't go with me to heaven.

When I die, my spirit and soul will go to heaven and my body will return to dust. I'll receive my new heavenly body. My soul will go to heaven in the state in which it had been sanctified through the binding and loosing process in this life.

Here is scripture that supports this truth.

> According to the grace of God which was given to me, as a wise master-builder I laid a foundation and another is building upon it. But let each man be careful how he builds upon it. For no man can lay a foundation other than the one which is laid, which is Jesus Christ. Now if any man builds upon the foundation with gold, silver, precious stones, wood, hay, straw, each man's work will become evident; for the day will show it, because it is to be revealed with fire; and the fire itself will test the quality of each man's work. If any man's work which he has built upon remains, he shall receive a reward. If any man's work is burned up, he shall suffer loss; but he himself shall be saved, yet so as through fire. (1 Corinthians 3:10–15)

Salvation is not a question; the question is what I built my life on this earth with—gold, silver, and precious stones are God's building materials—and what He asked me or showed me to do. John 5:19 reads, "Truly, truly, I say to you, the Son can do nothing of Himself, unless it is something He sees the Father doing; for whatever the Father does, these things the Son also does in like manner."

Wood, hay, and straw are materials that originate in my soul, the part of me still being influenced by the laws of sin and death—my old nature being led by what I call the three s's: self, sin, and Satan. That is what is burned up as we enter heaven. I don't lose my salvation because I'm still in heaven, but I will suffer loss. I don't know how this works out in heaven, but I will find out when I get there.

Here are some scriptures that have encouraged me in my walk in the Spirit over the last forty-five years.

And we know that God causes all things to work for good to those who love God, to those who are called according to His purpose. For whom He foreknew, He also predestined to become conformed to the image of His Son, that He might be the first-born among many brethren; and whom He predestined, these He also called; and whom He called, these He also justified; and whom He justified, these He also glorified. (Romans 8:28–30)

To be glorified means to bring into existence God's plan for my life now.

For we are His workmanship, created in Christ Jesus for good works, which God prepared beforehand, that we should walk in them. (Ephesians 2:10)

For I know the plans that I have for you, declares the Lord, plans for welfare and not for calamity to give you a future and a hope. (Jeremiah 29:11)

CHAPTER 3

Seeing and Hearing

Mark 8:18 reads, "Having eyes, do you not see? And having ears, do you not hear?"

We are also told,

> He who has ears, let him hear. And the disciples came and said to Him, "Why do you speak to them in parables? And He answered and said to them, "to you it has been granted to know the mysteries (revelation) of the kingdom of Heaven, but to them it has not been granted. For whoever has, to him shall more be given, and he shall have an abundance; but whoever does not have, even what he has shall be taken away from him. Therefore I speak to them in parables; because while seeing they do not see, and while hearing they do not hear, nor do they understand. And in their case the prophecy of Isaiah is being fulfilled, which says.

> You will keep on hearing, but will not understand; And you will keep on seeing, but will not perceive; For the heart of this people has become dull, And with their ears they scarcely hear, And they have closed their eyes; Lest they should see with their eyes, And hear with their ears, And understand with their heart and turn again, And I should heal them. But blessed are your eyes, because they see; and your ears, because they hear. (Matthew 13:9–16)

I think there are two classes of people in the church—those who have been granted the ability to see and hear, and those who have not been granted that ability. The former continue to receive revelation, but the latter have just education, not revelation, and it is burned up when they go to heaven. The Holy Spirit was not the source of what they understand.

We read in Colossians 2:11, "In Him you were also circumcised with a circumcision made without hands, in the removal of the body of the flesh by the circumcision of Christ." That is the result of Pentecost that first came to the apostles in Acts 1–2. The baptism of the Holy Spirit gives the power that separates the soul from the spirit, and spiritual seeing and hearing become clear—no fuzziness anymore about spiritual truth. Acts 1:8 reads, "But you shall receive power when (after) the Holy Spirit has come upon you; and you shall be My witnesses (sample) both in Jerusalem, and in all Judea and Samaria, and even to the remotest part of the earth."

> Yet we do speak wisdom among those who are mature; a wisdom, however, not of this age, nor of the rulers of this age, who are passing away; but we speak God's wisdom in a mystery, the hidden wisdom, which God predestined before the ages to our glory; the wisdom which none of the rulers of

this age has understood; for if they had understood it, they would not have crucified the Lord of glory; but just as it written; (Isaiah, the Prophet): "Things which eye has not seen and ear has not heard, and which have not entered the heart of man, All that God has prepared for those who love Him.

For to us God revealed them through the Spirit; for the Spirit searches all things, even the depths of God. For who among men knows the thoughts of a man except the spirit of the man, which is in him? Even so the thoughts of God no one knows except the Spirit of God. Now we have received, not the spirit of the world, but the Spirit who is from God, that we might know the things freely given to us by God, which things we speak, not in words taught by human wisdom, but those taught by the Spirit, combining spiritual thoughts with spiritual words. But a natural man does not accept the things of the Spirit of God; for they are foolishness to him, and he cannot understand them, because they are spiritually appraised. But he who is spiritual appraises all things, yet he himself is appraised by no man. For who has known the mind of the Lord, that he should instruct Him? But we have the mind of Christ." (1 Corinthians 2:6–16)

Matthew 11:15 says, "He who has ears to hear, let him hear."

Some of my personal testimony follows and it is scripturally spoken of in Acts 2:17–Joel's prophesy.

And it shall be in the last days, God says, That I will pour forth of My Spirit upon all mankind; And your sons and your daughters shall prophecy, And your young men shall see visions, And your old men shall dream dreams.

As an old man (in my old nature), I had a dream and as a young man (in Christ) I have had many visions where the Holy Spirit has taught and directed my path as I continue to walk in the light of His Truth.

CHAPTER 4

The Nakedness Principle

When I worked in corporate sales in the late 1960s, I commuted to my office in New York only once or twice a week. My sales territory covered three states, so I was on the road most of the time. When I did go into the city, I parked on the west side of Manhattan and walked across 42nd Street to my office on the East Side.

In the 1960s, many adult bookstores lined 42nd Street. I had never been interested in going into one anywhere, but after several weeks of passing these stores, I ventured into one out of curiosity. I felt like a fish that had been hooked and was being reeled in. I know now that the lust of my flesh ruled my decision to go in.

I started buying paperbacks and would throw them away after reading them. I would never think of bringing them into my house; I kept that all to myself. That was the time I purchased my first issue of *Playboy* magazine. I would bring issues home, but I would hide them from my children. I don't remember if they ever found them, but they probably did.

As I have related in my born-again testimony, my life had been so changed for the better that I had thought my entering the world of pornography would never come up again in my walk. How wrong I was. My mind was bombarded with thoughts that I would resist, but they would come back often. I was not gaining victory over my thought life. I did not share this battle with my wife; I was too ashamed to let her know what was going on in my mind. I fought this battle by changing my thoughts, asking for prayer at many meetings, and even submitting to prayers for deliverance. That went on for seven years but without relief.

At this time, I was very involved with FGBMFI—The Full Gospel Businessman's Fellowship International Organization. A few of my friends and I traveled to an advance—we didn't call them retreats—in another city. It was a great weekend of fellowship, music, sharing, teaching, and prayer.

After meetings had concluded one day, I was alone in my room resting and peaceful after a full day of involvement with the things of the Lord. I heard the Holy Spirit say to me, "Do you want to be free from your bondage?" I exclaimed, "What do you mean do I want to be free? You know I've asked to be delivered from this bondage for seven years!" In a calm but powerful voice, He said, "Get your Bible. Open it to Genesis 2. Read verse 24."

I did. I read, "For this cause a man shall leave his father and his mother, and shall cleave to his wife; and they shall become one flesh."

The Holy Spirit asked me, "What does your flesh include?" I said that my flesh was the combination of my soul and body. He said, "That's correct. And I want you to know that when you have intercourse with your wife, you are joined bodily and with your souls—your minds, emotions, and wills. When you separate bodily, your souls remain attached as one—you have a soul tie with your wife. That's my plan to strengthen your marriage relationship. You become soul mates by my design. Read verse 25."

I did. "And the man and his wife were both naked and were not ashamed." The word *ashamed* jumped off the page because that had been what had kept me from being open with my wife. "You haven't been open with your wife concerning your battle with pornographic thoughts. When you go home, share or be open with your wife about your mind problem and you will be free."

I couldn't wait to get home and share with my wife what the Lord had told me. She listened and wasn't at all embarrassed or critical of my past behavior; she just thanked the Lord for freeing me from my bondage. From that point on in our walk with the Lord, we referred to this principle as getting naked together, that is, keeping our minds open to each other.

That happened over forty years ago. We tried to live up to that principle, but other areas of separation were not resolved before my Annie went home to be with the Lord. I am remorseful about that; I grieve for that and have been working it out with the Lord since her passing.

This soul-tie truth is something I have never heard from any Christian teacher or source. But I know the truth of it and teach it to the inmates at the correctional facility where I have been teaching for the last twelve years. I explain this truth to inmates and point out what James 1:8 says: "… being a double-minded man, unstable in all his ways."

There is such infidelity among men and women today because they are torn emotionally and being pulled in all directions due to the physical relationships they have had. We don't have to look far to see that this is an epidemic in the world today.

The Lord has also assured me that if someone is truly convicted by the Holy Spirit about this sin and sincerely confesses and asks forgiveness, He will grant it. Matthew 26:28 reads, "For this is My blood of the covenant, which is to be shed on behalf of many for the forgiveness of sins."

CHAPTER 5

The Battlefield of the Mind

Ephesians 6:12 tells us,

> For our struggle is not against flesh and blood, but against the rulers, against the powers, against the world-forces of this darkness, against the spiritual forces of wickedness in the heavenly places.

The Lord set me free of the unclean thoughts I had been captive to, but Satan has always attempted to get back into my thought life. I've fought this spiritual battle with spiritual tools—the scriptures.

What Satan does is found in Revelation 12:9–10.

> And the great dragon was thrown down, the serpent of old who is called the Devil and Satan, who deceives the whole world; he was thrown down to the earth, and his angels were thrown down with him. And I heard a loud voice in heaven, saying, Now the salvation, and the power, and the kingdom of our God and the authority of His Christ have come, for

the accuser of our brethren has been thrown down, who accuses them before our God day and night.

I have to take control of my thoughts; God will not. Satan has free access to my thoughts and does so through his darts of temptations and unclean thoughts to entice me into his domain.

These scriptures have always helped me in this ongoing battle. I have memorized and sometimes sing the first one here.

> I will bless the Lord at all times; His praise shall continually be in my mouth. My soul shall make its boast in the Lord; The humble shall hear it and rejoice. O magnify the Lord with me, And let us exalt His name together. I sought the Lord, and He answered me, And delivered me from all my fears. (Psalm 34:1–4)

> Set your mind on the things above, not on the things that are on earth. (Colossians 3:2)

> We are destroying speculations and every lofty thing raised up against the knowledge of God, and we are taking every thought captive to the obedience of Christ. (2 Corinthians 10:5)

I have always been encouraged by the power of faith in the scriptures. After Jesus was baptized by John and was led by the Spirit into the wilderness to be tempted by the devil, He spoke these powerful words to Satan in response to Satan's temptations: "It is written ..." and then He quoted scriptures. Matthew 4:11 states, "Then the devil left Him; and behold angels came and began to minister to Him."

CHAPTER 6

Angels

Psalm 91:11–12 teaches of the one who trusts in the Lord: "For He will give His angels charge concerning you, to guard you in all your ways. They will bear you up in their hands, lest you strike your foot against a stone."

Angels have been a part of my spiritual walk for over forty-five years. I post them on the four corners of my car when I drive anywhere. I post them on the corners of my house when I leave for a time. I have seen angels several times; here are two of my experiences.

This is from Ann's notes in her journal.

> Near the end of my mother's life, she was hospitalized with pneumonia. As her body weakened, her very wise and loving doctor explained to us that Mom had only about one more week to live. Because Mom wasn't suffering, Bruce and I felt to go home one night for some needed rest. I tried to sleep, but as I pictured Mom alone in her hospital bed, I felt an overwhelming sadness and was filled with anxiety. I asked Bruce if he would pray for me and as he did, the following happened:

Bruce: As I was praying for the peace of the Lord to fill Ann's heart, the Lord gave me a vision of Mom in her hospital bed and just above her head, at each bedpost, were angels dressed all in white standing guard over Mom as she was sleeping. These "Guardian Angels" remained in their same position each time I looked—both while we were there at bedside or away in another place; I could close my eyes and see the vision God had given me. I would always share with Ann, each time I saw the angels.

Ann: My heart was filled with gratitude for God's powerful love reaching down to care for Mom and to comfort our hearts! As we shared our time with Mom, each day I would ask Bruce: are the angels still there? And he would answer yes. And there came the last day when our family encircled Mom's bed, holding hands and praying silently as her physical life ebbed away. The angels were gone—with Mom—ushering her into her heavenly home!

Another visitation of angels happened at Bible school. We were having a very powerful time of worship that went on for several minutes. As I lifted my hands in praise, I opened my eyes and saw a band of angels gathered in the air above. They had come to hear and observe the songs and words of praise we were lifting to heaven. I smiled and whispered, "Thank you, Lord."

CHAPTER 7

The Meat Hook Principle

In the first years after the dream and my "born of the Spirit" experience, my real estate business was running into cash-flow problems. My solution was to borrow money on a short-term basis to meet payroll and other immediate expenses. I had an idea of what income would be available soon, so I felt comfortable borrowing from a bank. But in my morning quiet time with the Lord, I started feeling uncomfortable about borrowing money. I remembered a Christian friend had once said that if he didn't have money, he wouldn't borrow to buy something.

One morning during my quiet time, the Lord gave me a vision. I saw a chalkboard in front of me, and a stick man began to form on the board—a circle for the head, a larger circle for the body, and stick arms and legs. In the upper left corner was a hand holding a meat hook. It started ripping into the middle circle, the body of the figure. The man grabbed the hand that held the meat hook and said, "That's my flesh! Don't take it!" The arm disappeared. But the same arm with the meat hook moved down from the upper right corner and ripped into the middle circle; at the top of the chalkboard were the words "It's Me" and Matthew 22:14: "For many are called, but few are chosen." Added for me was, "for the deeper walk." The man in the vision relaxed and let his flesh be ripped away.

I knew I was supposed to change my business practice of borrowing money. From then on, if we didn't have it, we didn't spend it, and the business went on following that principle.

And the principle of allowing my thoughts and ideas to prevail slowly changed as I began to hear the Lord's direction from my spirit more clearly. Two scriptures that are cross-references to Matthew 22:14 encouraged me in my walk.

> These will wage war against the Lamb, and the Lamb will overcome them, because He is Lord of lords and King of kings, and those who are with Him are the called and chosen and faithful. (Revelation 17:14)

> Therefore, brethren, be all the more diligent to make certain about His calling and choosing you; for as long as you practice these things, you will never stumble; for in this way the entrance into the eternal kingdom of our Lord and Savior Jesus Christ will be abundantly supplied to you. (2 Peter 1:10–11)

Remember, the kingdom of our Lord and Savior Jesus Christ is an experience for now!

CHAPTER 8

The Promised Land

In the Old Testament, the Promised Land was a piece of real estate called the land of Canaan. Joshua was chosen to lead the sons of Israel into this land. Joshua 1:1–3 reads,

> Now it came about after the death of Moses the servant of the Lord that the Lord spoke to Joshua the son of Nun, Moses' servant, saying, Moses My servant is dead; now therefore arise, cross this Jordan, you and all this people, to the land which I am giving to them, to the sons of Israel. Every place on which the sole of your foot treads, I have given it to you, just as I spoke to Moses.

The land was filled with seven nations that were the Israelites' enemies and had to be destroyed. Deuteronomy 7:16 reads, "And you shall consume all the peoples whom the Lord your God will deliver to you; your eye shall not pity them, neither shall you serve their gods, for that would be a snare to you."

The Lord has shown me that on this side of the cross, the Promised Land is the souls of Christians who have been saved, born of water.

My soul, the Promised Land, must do battle with its enemies also. Here is a list of the nations we must destroy. I made a note of these nations over forty years ago, but I didn't write down the source or I would have given it credit. What I do know is that the Holy Spirit confirmed that He was the original source, so I'll give Him the credit.

Before listing the nations, here is some more history regarding Joshua and the Israelites. They had to be circumcised since they had not been when they were in the wilderness for forty years. Then they were ready to do battle in the Promised Land as they were led by the Lord.

What accomplishes this for Christians today is found in Colossians 2:11: "In Him you were also circumcised with a circumcision made without hands, in the removal of the body of the flesh by circumcision of Christ" This happened to me in my dream—my soul was separated from my spirit so I could see things of the spiritual realm clearly. I was baptized in the Holy Spirit or born of the Spirit.

Nations in Our Souls to Be Destroyed
1. emotional problems—anger, fear, self-pity
2. mental problems—torment, confusion, double-mindedness
3. speech problems—cursing, blasphemy, gossip
4. sex problems—lust, fornication, adultery, pornography
5. addictions—alcohol, drugs, food
6. physical infirmities
7. religious errors—cults, the occult, false doctrines

The instructions given the Israelites in Deuteronomy 7:17–24 apply to us today.

> If you should say in your heart, These nations are greater than I; how can I dispossess them? You shall not be afraid of them; you shall remember what the

Lord your God did to Pharaoh and to all Egypt: the great trials which your eyes saw and the signs and the wonders and the mighty hand and the outstretched arm by which the Lord your God brought you out. So shall the Lord your God do to all the peoples of whom you are afraid. Moreover, the Lord your God will send the hornet against them, until those who are left and hide themselves from you, perish. You shall not dread them, for the Lord your God is in your midst, a great and awesome God. And the Lord your God will clear away these nations before you little by little; you will not be able to put an end to them quickly, lest the wild beasts grow too numerous for you. But the Lord your God shall deliver them before you, and will throw them into great confusion until they are destroyed. And He will deliver their kings into your hand so that you shall make their name perish from under heaven; no man will be able to stand before you until you have destroyed them.

This is my personal testimony about a nation I never completely defeated until my precious Annie went home to be with the Lord. It's in the addiction nation, and it's alcohol. Ann and I heard from the Lord through 2 Timothy 4:2—"Be ready in season and out of season"—soon after my dream when I had been baptized in the Holy Spirit. We understood that I was to give up all alcohol, and I did. That lasted for several years, but it slowly crept back in as I began to rationalize with myself that a beer after playing golf on a summer day was okay. And then an occasional cocktail when dining out or at a party. I stopped again for a while, but then, I began listening to those who said one or two drinks a day were okay for a man. None of this was wisdom from above; it was just my own reasoning.

When we were first married, Ann and I had an understanding that if the two of us didn't agree on something, we wouldn't do it until we did agree. I broke that agreement a number of times. But the most destructive non-agreement involved alcohol. An important scripture in this regard is found in 1 Corinthians 11:12: "For as the woman originates from the man, so also the man has his birth through the woman." The Lord let me know that I had had my birth through a woman and had a continual birthing or growing in the Spirit through a woman—my wife. She was a reflection of my spiritual condition. She was a responder to what I said or did in our relationship. She liked to say that I held the umbrella as covering and that she came under it next to me for protection.

One of her journal entries explains how she had been affected by my disobedience in this area.

> When alcohol is part of the equation, I see that I lose Bruce & the clear headed channel for Your Word to come through. I feel there is another power in control and anything can happen. There is not the peace inside me that You are in control. When Bruce, as your representative to the family—a steady hand at the helm of the ship—is not in control, I am "out there" on my own. There is no check to what is said— no one is in charge—that authority, that level head of the priest & prophet is missing (absent, unaware). The alcohol relaxes, dulls responsibility and the enemy has an "in" to cause family separations.
>
> The wife is the reflection of the spiritual condition of the man. I feel insecure and anxious—not knowing or being able to rest in the assurance that my whole Bruce, as God's representative to our family, is in

charge—the weariness as I try to keep up but feeling out from under any covering.

Writing and reading these words of hers brings grief and sadness back, but now, I have the opportunity to tell you what the Holy Spirit has accomplished in my life regarding my alcohol addiction since her homegoing last year.

I was invited to dinner with good friends, John and Dianne, the month after Ann's passing. We shared about Ann for an hour or so as we enjoyed cocktails before dinner. Later that evening after a great dinner and fellowship, I was putting on my coat and shoes. As I bent over to tie my shoes, I felt my blood pressure rising in my head, and blood began to drip from my nose. I quickly got some tissues and attempted to plug my nose. On the way home, I heard loudly and clearly "No more alcohol!" I knew who was speaking.

That was a bad night; I didn't get much sleep as I attempted to get the bleeding stopped. I had the greatest awareness of being alone without my nurse wife, Ann. I don't think I had ever felt so downhearted and lonesome—truly all alone.

Several days passed before I thought I had gotten things under control. But then one night, it started again. Out of desperation, I asked, "Lord, what should I do?"

That second, John, the person I had had dinner with that night, came to my mind. I called him and asked if he would take me to the emergency room. I told him my nose was bleeding again and I couldn't stop it. He arrived within minutes and drove me to the hospital. We waited for hours for a doctor to see me, but the bleeding had stopped, so we drove home at daylight.

I had two appointments with an ear, nose, and throat specialist, and eventually, everything seemed to be back to normal with my nose. By then, I had had time to ask the Lord about the incident, and I heard Him say, "I sent the hornet." I knew what He was referring to—Deuteronomy 7:20: "Moreover, the Lord your God will send the hornet against them, until those who are left and hide themselves from you, perish." The king of the alcohol demons had been exposed and defeated.

I'm reminded of a truth I learned years ago: if you don't hear the still, soft voice of the Holy Spirit in the intuition of your spirit, He will place the talking donkey in your path or send you off with Jacob's limp. Well, the hornet He had sent my way was that bleeding nose, and He certainly got my attention and ongoing obedience to His dictate: "No more alcohol!"

Thank you, Lord Jesus!

CHAPTER 9

Communion

John 6:48–58 reads,

> I am the bread of life. Your fathers ate the manna in the wilderness, and they died. This is the bread which comes down out of heaven; if any one eats of this bread, he shall live forever; and the bread also which I shall give for the life of the world is My flesh. The Jews therefore began to argue with one another, saying, "How can this man give us His flesh to eat?" Jesus therefore said to them, "Truly, truly, I say to you, unless you eat the flesh of the Son of Man and drink His blood, you have no life in yourselves. "He who eats My flesh and drinks My blood has eternal life; and I will raise him up on the last day. For My flesh is true food, and My blood is true drink. He who eats My flesh and drinks My blood abides in Me, and I in him. As the living Father sent Me, and I live because of the Father; so he who eats Me, he also shall live because of Me. This is the bread which

came down out of heaven; not as the fathers ate, and died; he who eats this bread shall live forever."

Revelation 3:20–22 tells us,

> Behold, I stand at the door and knock; if any one hears My voice and opens the door, I will come into him, and will dine with him, and he with Me. He who overcomes, I will grant to him to sit down with Me on My throne, as I overcame and sat down with My Father on His throne. He who has an ear, let him hear what the Spirit says to the churches.

We pray in the Lord's prayer, "Give us this day our daily bread." The bread we are asking for is not natural but spiritual food. Jesus's flesh is true food. The door being knocked on is the door between my spirit and soul. The handle is on my soul's side only. I must open it and invite Him in to dine with me, that is, to be involved with my daily walk. I can then overcome, sit with Him, and know I have a Helper for the trials and tribulations life offers.

That's how we eat His flesh and drink His blood as we take heed to John's word in 1 John 1:7: "But if we walk in the light as He Himself is in the light, we have fellowship with one another, and the blood of Jesus His Son cleanses us from all sin."

An idea that has been impressed on me is that the Christian walk is a daily walk—actually, it's a moment-by-moment walk.

> We are apt to imagine that if Jesus Christ constrains us, and we obey Him, He will lead us to great success. We must never put our dreams of success as God's purpose for us; His purpose may be exactly the opposite. We have an idea that God is leading us to a particular end, a desired goal; He is not. The

question of getting to a particular end is a mere incident. What we call the process, God calls the end.

What is my dream of God's purpose? His purpose is that I depend on Him and on His power now. If I can stay in the middle of the turmoil calm and unperplexed, that is the end of the purpose of God. God is not working towards a particular finish; His end is the process---that I see Him walking on the waves, no shore in sight, no success, no goal, just the absolute certainty that it is all right because I see Him walking on the sea. It is the process, not the end, which is glorifying to God.

God's training is for now, not presently. His purpose is for this minute, not for something in the future. We have nothing to do with the afterwards of obedience; we get wrong when we think of the afterwards. What men call training and preparation, God calls the end.

God's end is to enable me to see that He can walk on the chaos of my life just now. If we have a further end in view, we do not pay sufficient attention to the present: if we realize that obedience is the end, then each moment as it comes is precious. (OC, July 28)

In conclusion, we eat and drink spiritual food every minute of every day if we make the right choice about whom we serve.

Matthew 6:24 reads, "No one can serve two masters; for either he will hate the one and love the other, or he will hold to one and despise the other. You cannot (are unable) to serve God and Mammon."

CHAPTER 10

My Hiding Place

During one of our gatherings for fellowship, one woman asked for prayer. As was our practice, we put a chair in the center of the room for her and gather, laid hands on, and prayed for the Lord's wisdom to come forth. She asked to be released from the anxieties and fears that occupied her mind.

As we waited on the Lord, a few people spoke words of encouragement. A vision began appearing in my mind. I started to talk about what I was seeing.

I saw a woman standing with her arms crossed in front of her body. Her face was looking up, and her expression was not peaceful. I noticed she was standing in a black box that looked like it was made of concrete. I saw a banner above her head that read, "My Hiding Place." I saw her arms raised; she was praising God. Then, I saw her out of the box and standing in a shallow pool of water. Her face was radiant, and she was full of praise for the Lord. The banner above her head then read, "Come unto Me."

We then talked about what she was experiencing; she said she had released all her fears to the Lord. Someone quoted 1 Peter 5:7: "… casting all your anxiety upon Him, because He cares for you."

I mentioned that water signified eternal life, the same power Jesus walked in during His time on earth.

Someone read from Luke 4:18 that quotes Isaiah's prophecy.

> The Spirit of the Lord is upon me, because He has sent Me to proclaim release to the captives, and recovery of sight to the blind, to set free those who are downtrodden, to proclaim the favorable year of the Lord.

This is an appropriate place to quote again George Warnock's statement that I have in the prologue.

> If this is the day of the unveiling of Christ, and the joining together of the Body of Christ, it is also the day of the UNVEILING OF THE HUMAN HEART, and the manifestation of the hidden things of darkness that lie concealed in the hearts of God's people.

CHAPTER 11

Gold and Silver Nuggets

- Spiritual authority is recognized and voluntarily submitted to; it is never to be imposed on anyone.
- Spiritual truth is heard first in the intuition of our spirits and then in our minds.
- The church has no existence apart from the revelation of Jesus Christ.
- More important than what we are doing is what we are becoming.
- We are coming out of the church age and into the kingdom age.
- We are called to the Tree of Life, not to the Tree of Good and Evil.
- The willing and obedient will inherit the good of the land.
- We are called to be ruled by the Holy Spirit now so we can rule with Him in eternity.
- "That which proceeds from a wounded soul is filthy" (Pat Robertson, CBN).
- Grace is the God-given energizing to do His will.
- We are in the final days of preparation.
- His presence precedes His person.

CHAPTER 12

Baptized With The Holy Spirit

In Matthews 3:11 He writes that John the Baptist says: "As for me, I baptize you in water from repentance; but He who is coming after me is mightier than I, and I am not even fit to remove His sandals; He Himself will baptize you with the Holy Spirit and fire.

And His winnowing fork in His hand, and He will thoroughly clean His threshing floor; and He will gather His wheat into the barn, but He will burn up the chaff with unquenchable fire,"

Spiritually speaking, His threshing floor is my soul (mind, emotions and will), in which He arranges circumstances that expose myself, sin and Satan influenced traits that He will burn up with His fire. This is done little by little for the rest of my days on earth. It can be called sanctification.

In John Chapter 3:5 John writes: "Jesus answered, Truly, truly, I say to you, unless one is born of water and the Spirit, he cannot (is not able) enter the kingdom of God."

The water Jesus is talking about is "living water" which enables initial salvation and is identified by Jesus and stated in John:7:37-39 which reads: " Now on the last day, the great day of the feast, Jesus stood and cried out saying, If any man is thirsty, let him come to Me and drink. He who believes in Me, as the Scripture said, "From his innermost (his spirit) being shall flow rivers of living water. But this He spoke of the Spirit, whom those who believed in Him were to receive; for the Spirit was not yet given, because Jesus was not yet glorified."

In conclusion, being born of water is initial salvation, when the Holy Spirit enters my spirit and born of the Spirit is when my soul is baptized with the Holy Spirit. I can then, enter the kingdom of God, which is an earthly experience for now. In Luke Chapter 17:20 & 21 Luke writes: " Now having been questions by the Pharisees as to when the kingdom of God was coming, He answered them and said "The kingdom of God is not coming with signs to be observed; nor will they say, 'Look, here it is!' or 'There it is!' For behold, thy kingdom of God is in your midst."(within you).

There are several examples of the spiritual birthing experience in the Book of Acts that follow the same sequence.

Acts Chapter 8:14-17 Reads: "Now when the apostles in Jerusalem heard that Samaria had received the word of God, they sent them Peter and John, who came down and prayed for them, that they might receive the Holy Spirit. For He had not fallen upon them; they had simply been baptized in the name of Jesus. Then they began laying their hands on them, and they were receiving the Holy Spirit.

Acts Chapter 10:44-47 Reads: "While Peter was still speaking these words, the Holy Spirit fell upon those who were listening to the message. And all the circumcised believers who had come with Peter were amazed, because the gift of the Holy Spirit had been poured out upon the Gentiles also. For they were hearing them speaking with tongues and exalting God. Then Peter answered, Surely no one can refuse the water for these to be baptized who have received the Holy Spirit just as we did, can he? And he ordered them to be baptized in the name of Jesus Christ. Then they asked him to stay on for a few days."

Grip of Heaven

Acts Chapter 19:17 Reads:" And it came about that while Apollos was at Corinth, Paul having passed through the upper country came to Ephesus, and found some disciples, and he said to them, "Did you receive the Holy Spirit when you believed?" And they said to him, "No, we have not even heard whether there is a Holy Spirit." And he said, "Into what then were you baptized?" And they said, "Into John's baptism," And Paul said, "John baptized with the baptism of repentance, telling the people to believe in Him who was coming after him, that is, in Jesus." And when they heard this, they were baptized in the name of Jesus. And when Paul had laid his hands upon them, the Holy Spirit came on them, and they began speaking with tongues and prophesying. And there were in all about twelve men."

In closing this chapter of this book, I'd like to bring you a section of a book entitled" Baptism In The Holy Spirit written by Derek Prince, back in 1964, on page 29, in section entitled "For Unity".

"Finally I go back to my initial verse, 1 Corinthians 12:13: "In one spirit we were baptized in to one body." Remember the unifying purpose of God in baptizing believers in the Holy Ghost. It is not to separate them, it is to unite them. Somebody complained in the United States about certain church where the minister had been baptized in the Holy Spirit and some of the congregation had gone along with him, while others had not: "The trouble with this experience is, it's dividing the church." To this a minister I know gave this answer, and I think it is a good answer. He said "Well, that's remarkable, because in the early church it had exactly the opposite effect. When the Jews heard the Gentiles speak with other tongues, it was the only thing that united Jews and Gentiles in one church, and nothing else would have done it." Likewise, I tell you today that the only thing that will bring Baptists and Plymouth Brethren and Assemblies of God and Anglicans and Lutherans and Presbyterians and ten other different denominations together in large numbers, embracing one another, throwing their arms up in the air, spending half an hour doing nothing but praise God---there is only one thing that will do that, the baptism in the Holy Ghost."

And I add my Amen to that!

A PRAYER

Jesus, I thank you for saving me and regenerating my spirit and now, I ask you to baptize me with your Holy Spirit, as I place my soul, with its life of self, sin and Satan's influence on the alter, for You to burn up this chaff with Your unquenchable fire. Thank you Jesus---You are now my Lord and Savior with your heart's desire that my soul be conformed to Your image. Amen!

www.ingramcontent.com/pod-product-compliance
Lightning Source LLC
Chambersburg PA
CBHW060413080526
44583CB00012B/548